"CASINO CRAPS
is a Vicious
$$ Devouring Game"

Zeke Feinberg

All correspondence and inquiries should be directed to
Reference Division,
Hi-Lo-Yo Publishing
P.O. Box 711
Skippack, PA 19474-0711

Library of Congress Cataloging in Publication Data Main entry under title: "CASINO CRAPS IS A VICIOUS $$ DEVOURING GAME"

Library of Congress Catalog Card Number: 92-081657
ISBN: 1-881174-03-4

Printed in the United States of America

You Can Win
and Earn Profits
Playing Casino Craps

New,
Never Before Disclosed
Methods to Avoid
Devastating Sevens

Zeke Feinberg

This book was
written in
SPITE OF MANY

The Author

CASINO CRAPS IS A VICIOUS $$ DEVOURING GAME

TABLE OF CONTENTS

"Cutting The Crap Out Of Craps"

Most enthusiastic Casino CRAP players have no patience or desire to allow a 200 page book on CRAPS delay their entrance into the exhilarating, fascinating, entertaining and mystifying arena of CRAP action.

Therefore:
Let's cut the crap and quickly tell it in eighty pages.

For more detailed information and arithmetic proof obtain this author's book "Earn $12 to $24 Per Hour Playing Casino CRAPS."

CASINO CRAPS IS A VICIOUS GAME

The casino's win percentage as represented by the New Jersey Casino Commission is approximately fifteen (15 %).

This fifteen (15 %) casino's win percentage is based on actual gross amount of cash and markers exchanged for gambling chips. The net amount of actual money exposed to the exciting, exhilarating game of craps is substantially less. (See article in this book about "Casinos Devour Over 34 % of the CRAP Bankroll"). This will explain the 'true drop'.

According to a fourteen month study by this author, the actual casino's win percentage of true drop exceeds 34 %.

WHY ?

The answer became obvious when I decided to study the *Game Of Casino Craps.*

Every author who has ever written about this fantastic exciting game recommends the identical methods to "win at Casino CRAPS".

They all repeat the identical garbage. If all these authors

agree on how to win at Casino CRAPS, then someone ought to explain why less than 1 % of Casino Craps players are overall winners.

The late John Scarne was the very best author and expert on all phases of gambling. His books, especially on DICE, inspired me to further investigate the game of CRAPS. Personally, I treasure his superb books on all types of gambling.

Okay, if you are satisfied to grind for **profit,** we can now proceed.

These methods can be applied to any size wagers to reap profits.

I like to consider my techniques as *not gambling*, but more like *grinding the Casinos* for profit.

This author is the only CRAP author to state *"The only way to win at casino Craps is through the *green pastures of the Place bets".*

As of this writing no one has developed a system or technique to win overall in the Arena of CRAP action. No one has put forth a workable money management system to win overall in Casino CRAPS.

* As in Green Dollar Signs.

That is why approximately five to eight out of a thousand CRAP players are overall winners. *This is less than 1 %.*

This means, that as of April 1992, there were 214 CRAP tables in the twelve Atlantic City Casinos. Most of these CRAP tables hold 12 *potential losers*. The fewer large CRAP tables allow 16 *almost non-existent winners* to participate in the exciting Palladium of CRAP Action.

Less than 2700 CRAP players are needed to have 100 % capacity at any one given moment. Of these 2700 potential victims of those dazzlin' DICE, only 81, or 3 %, would leave the casinos as winners. This equates to 97 % of the players lose their bankroll because they are uneducated in the Arena of CRAP Action. As these same 81 players play another day, or later sessions during the year, the overall winners will dwindle to about 24 from the original 2700. This is less than 1 % of our theoretical 2700.

The Hippodrome of Casino CRAPS is a dying gambling game. This is evidenced by the fact that before Donald Trump's Taj Mahal, the total number of CRAP tables in Atlantic City approached 250. The Taj Mahal added 30 more CRAP tables,

BUT

the total has dwindled to only 214. The Bally Grand and others are removing CRAP tables to make room for additional slot machines. Soon there will be less than 200 CRAP tables in Atlantic City.

In Las Vegas most casinos have few CRAP tables. Steve Wynn's Mirage has 12 CRAP tables. Caesar's Palace has 13 CRAP tables. Many others have only one, two or three.

There are two reasons why this exhilarating game of CRAPS shows declining trends.

First Reason:

A miniscule percentage of casino personnel and CRAP players really understand Casino CRAPS. This equates to less than 1 % of the Casino personnel able to give you a correct answer to specific question on the finer points of CRAPS.

Second Reason:

Casino CRAPS is a very fast, confusing game. Old timers learned CRAPS in the streets and in the armed services. The younger generation cannot cope with the variety of wagers and the speed of the game. No one can cope with the Casino CRAP'S appetite for devouring over 34 % of the players bankroll.

In a recent poll that I supervised, I asked 316 *Casino personnel two basic questions:

(a) What is the best wager in the Arena of CRAP Action ?

(b) Is it better to "buy" the place bets 4 or 10, or merely place bet the 4 or 10 if you intend pressing (increasing) these wagers when they become winners ?

Poll Results for (a) :

Pass Line Bet with Maximum Odds	87
Don't Pass Line Bet with Maximum Odds	229
Total Idiots	316

Poll Results for (b) :

"Buy" the 4 or 10	316
Place bet the 4 or 10	0
Total Imbeciles	316

Articles in this book will clearly explain that both the Pass Line and Don't Pass Line are **poor wagers.** The supposedly "true odds" is a trap for further transforming these **poor wagers** into **disastrous wagers.**

* Dealers, Box Persons, Floor Supervisors, Pit Managers, Shift Managers and top very highly paid Casino Executives.

Every other CRAP *auth*or (as in *auth*ority) stupidly claims the Pass Line and Don't Pass Line wagers are the very best in the Arena of CRAP action. They also state these wagers improve as you take or lay maximum odds. After reading the article in "Decreasing Percentages" you will understand why copy-cat authors are not the authority.

When making wagers on the Place bets 4 or 10 it is better to "buy" the first wager. To "buy" the 4 or 10 the player pays the casino a commission of 5% to obtain the true odds of 2 to 1, instead of 9 to 5. This is called vigorish in the Arena of CRAP action. The advantage on the first buy is less than 5% over Place betting the 4 or 10. After the very first win, the win factor increases dramatically in favor of Place betting the four or ten. As an example, compare the difference between "buying" the 4 or 10 and Place betting the 4 or 10. If a player is fortunate to overcome the odds of 728 to 1 for six fully pressed "buy" bets, compared to fully pressing the place bets, the advantage for the place bettor is 12.89 times greater than the "buy" bettor. Repeat: after beating the odds of 728 to 1 for winning six times on the 4 or 10, the financial return (per dollar invested) is thirteen times better for the Place bettor. This is thirteen hundred percent (1300 %) better. Every additional win further expands the Place bettor's advantage.

Not one person in the Arena of CRAP Action ever disclosed this fact. No one, not the authors, the experts or casino people even knew this fact.

Warning - this author *does not approve* of the 4 or 10 Place bets unless charting indicates a very rare wager is viable.

Repeat: CRAP Authors and Casino Personnel comprise the know-nothing-ism of the CRAPS society.

WHAT HAPPENS TO PLAYER'S CRAP BANKROLL ?

Percentage of CRAP bankroll *lost*	Percentage of Players
100 %	27 %
50 %	35 %
20 %	16 %
10 %	11 %
0 % (Breakeven)	8 %
** Winners	3 %
	100 %

Percentages were obtained over a period of 24 months by periodically asking various players what the final financial results were the last session they played Casino CRAPS. By session it is meant the total time a CRAP player spent during a particular visit to the Atlantic City casinos. In some cases, it was a weekend, a day or so, others varied from a few hours, four to six hours or in the case of novices, perhaps 15 to 40 minutes.

* Author's opinion. Please note that these percentages are not related to dollars loss.

** These are winners for a particular session.

Overall winners, during the course of time, *dwindle to less than one percent of all CRAP players.*

EIGHTEEN WAYS TO WIN
SIX WAYS TO LOOSE

The only wagers I am concerned with are the **Place bets.** In the course of this book it is my hope to convince you that these are the only bets you should make. *Forget the rest of the table !* If you are wagering the 5, 6, 8 & 9 Place bets there are **eighteen ways for you to win** and only **six ways to lose.** But this is only the beginning!

To fully understand this analysis, imagine that when both DICE are thrown by the shooter, one of the pair of DICE (singular of DICE is called a DIE) lands first while the second DIE lands a split second later.

Therefore, if the first DIE lands with the number 1 up, the only way to lose would be if the second DIE landed with the number 6 on the topmost surface. Assuming you have Place bets on the 5, 6, 8, & 9, if the second DIE landed with the number 4 or 5 on the topmost surface you would win on either the 5 or 6 Place bets. Therefore, there would be *two ways to win and only one way to lose.*

Following this scenario, when the first DIE lands with the other numbers up, you can easily follow the table on page 16 that shows a total of *EIGHTEEN WAYS TO WIN AND SIX WAYS TO LOSE*, for these four Place bets.

I can hear the so called CRAP experts state that there is additional money at stake.

My retort, "Baloney "! Read on for an explanation. I have yet to meet or hear about *an expert on the game of CRAPS* who really *understands* the game of CRAPS.

EIGHTEEN WAYS TO WIN, SIX WAYS TO LOSE

PLACE BETS: 5, 6, 8 & 9

1st Die	2nd Die Winners	Ways to Win	* 2nd Die Loser	Ways to Lose
1	4 - 5 * *	2	6	1
2	3 - 4 - 6 *	3	5	1
3	2 - 3 - 5 - 6	4	4	1
4	1 - 2 - 4 - 5	4	3	1
5	* 1 - 3 - 4	3	2	1
6	* * 2 - 3	2	1	1

Place Bet # = 5,6,8 & 9   18 Wins   Losses = 6

The remaining 12 possible numbers that can be thrown have NO EFFECT on the Place bets. They neither cause a win or a loss (2, 3, 11, 12, 4 & 10).

* There will be only one number on the second DIE to create a losing 7 total.

DIAMETRICALLY OPPOSITE

The ideas in this book are *diametrically opposite* to what is generally considered to be the proper way to play CRAPS. If these so called experts had a sure-fire way of winning they would probably not share it with the public.

My curiosity in CRAPS is as a mathematical hobby and my interests are diversified. My primary income is derived from the manufacturing of transportation equipment. While writing this book, I have obtained copyrights on three games and have applied for two patents involving the parameters of the Game of CRAPS.

Talk is cheap. The final test will be if you as a reader of this book can change your status from that of a constant *overall loser* to that of an *overall winner ! ! !*

Let me attempt to put you on the right path of winning.

Before we continue, let's analyze the Place Bet combinations using the technique just developed.

CRAP TABLE LAYOUT

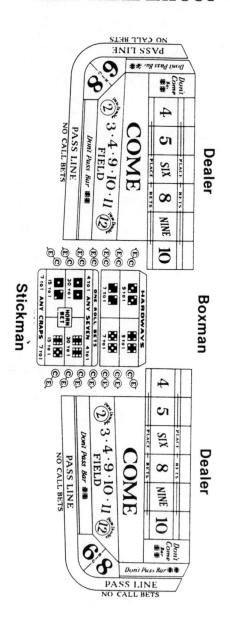

**NO BOOK ON THE GAME OF CRAPS
EVER DISCUSSED OR ANALYZED THE
VALUES OF THE CASINO'S PERCENTAGE
WHEN VARIOUS COMBINATIONS OF
PLACE BETS ARE MADE**

**OBVIOUSLY NO ONE EVER
INVESTIGATED THIS IMPORTANT
FACET OF THE GAME OF CRAPS.**

In fact, previous authors stated that combining wagers had no affect on Casino's win percentages. This is why these previous authors **never understood CRAPS!**

What to do for PLACE BETS
AFTER
Pass Line Winner makes new point.

This author is now adamant unless Pass Line winner has at least one 7 (natural) before a new or second Point is established - ***no wagers are to be made.*** I don't care if there are many additional pass line winners. I am satisfied to sit shooter out.

Even if the shooter is on one of those *most unusual hot streaks*, I don't care ! ! !

I am content to be an observer and charter. This is so rare a situation that in the long run I am better off by biding my time.

Even if pass line winner has a natural 7 on the come out roll, I may sit out the balance of the roll when glancing at a chart.

WARNING - MULTIPLE BETS

Also, when you win more than one place bet, the player has greater exposure in event of a loss (the 7 unexpectedly and undeservedly shows up).

The method of wagering multiple Place bets is *still safer* than pressing Place bets.

Additional Place bets add insurance to our casino attack, and with charting our insurance factor further increases.

PRESSING PLACE BETS

On an unusually long roll a player can increase his profitability dramatically by PRESSING the PLACE BETS.

I have witnessed successful long rolls, but disagree with this procedure. In the final analysis, the number of successful *'press the Place bets'* actions are greatly *outweighed by the losses.* This is due to the shorter rolls when measured in terms of dollars won and lost.

For every long profit making roll, there are too many short rolls that more than offset the advantage of the long roll.

True, you can be fortunate to play and press when this unusual successful long roll occurs, but in the final analysis, you will remain a *loser.*

They say

"Right Bettors Die Broke."

This author says

"Press Bettors Commit Financial Suicide."

If, as a CRAP player, you want to make a real fast killing by pressing place bets, then God bless you.

The *one time* you make a "killing" will more than be greatly offset by the *many, many times* you will lose ! ! !

$$\frac{\text{Loss Periods}}{\text{*Successful Exceptions}} \quad > \quad \frac{78}{1}$$

$$\frac{\text{**Loss Periods}}{\text{Successful Press Sessions}} \quad > \quad \frac{43}{1}$$

*Money making rolls continuing after making Place bets in the middle of unknown rolls. (Middle of unknown roll is indeterminate).

** Money making rolls when pressing place bets at outset of very first place bet win *after* establishing pass line point.

These values are from personal charting records.

DON'T BE GREEDY

DON'T PRESS PLACE BETS

INCREASE VALUES OF PLACE BETS AT OUTSET

when predicted by

CHARTING

SUPER-CHARTING

and MEGA-CHARTING

THE CRAP PLAYERS *UNKNOWN CURSE*

If you heard it once, you heard it hundreds of times.

> **"Dice have no memory and
> every toss or roll of the dice is
> completely independent of any previous
> toss of the dice."**

This is the *curse* of all CRAP players.

* Because of this curse *all* crap players have *lost* quite a bundle of chips !

* Whenever CRAP players approach a table in the middle of an unknown roll and make sizeable wagers they will be **doomed.**

WAIT

Another Friend Is Going
To Enhance Our
Chances Of Earning
Profits

CHARTING

This is the most important
singular chapter of this
book ! ! !

EVASION, YES AVOIDANCE

In order to be in a posture to win you will need all the tools available. Our attack on Casino CRAPS is actually an evasion *not an invasion*. Sounds contradictory !

A better choice of etymology would be *avoidance*.

Yes, avoidance.

This book will *not* assist you in playing CRAPS as it is **improperly played** in today's 'Arena of CRAP Action'. That's why there are over 99 % losers ! ! !

Forget any information you may have read or heard about the Game of CRAPS.

Our approach will be to find various methods, techniques and superstitions to avoid the 7's. This will minimize the appearance of those financially destructive 7's.

You will never eradicate the 7's. All you want to accomplish is simply obtain **four Place bet wins for ever singular losing 7.** Therefore our goal will be to avoid some of those critical 7's.

Besides being the most important chapter of this book, *CHARTING* is also the most prolific. Prior to re-writing the introduction to charting, 79 type-written pages on this subject were compiled plus an additional 40 odd handwritten pages.

Let's begin

Charting is compiling the flow of DICE numbers generated as the various shooters toss the DICE against the furthest padded wall.

Recall the CRAP Player's CURSE:

"Dice have no memory and every toss or roll of the dice is completely independent of any previous toss of the dice."

If the CRAP players curse is correct, can compiling the flow of past numbers assist us in projecting future outcomes ?

YES !

YES ! !

OH MY, YES ! ! !

CAN CHARTING REALLY HELP ?

How can previous charting be of any assistance ? This is a very fair and valid question.

If we were able to chart the CRAP action generated numbers for all the CRAP tables in the world for the next five or ten years, or go back in time and recapture the charting of all Las Vegas CRAP action for one day or 10 years, we would be amazed at the similarity of the charts.

These charts would include many of those once-in-a-lifetime so called *hot streaks.*

They would also include too many of those heart-breaking cold streaks (for the right bettors).

What does the charting REVEAL ?

By compiling the series of numbers generated by those intriguing DICE, certain predictions can be made. This will *minimize our loss periods* and **maximize our profit periods.**

This procedure is called CHARTING. Charting is accomplished by observing live CRAP action at the casinos. It also can be obtained by randomizing CRAP numbers on computers, or compiling numbers in the CRAP game called Pass Line CRAPS.

CHART READING

Chart reading is meant to be only *'glance read'*. **There is no need to study your chart.**

Just by 'glancing' at the chart you will gather sufficient information to act accordingly. A glance reader is as effective, as if the rolls generated were to be used as input to a high-tech computer. In this case, however, the computer is your brain.

NO COMPUTER CAN ACCURATELY PREDICT WHAT THE NEXT NUMBER OR NUMBERS GENERATED WILL BE TOSSED BY THE SHOOTER.

Your glance reading will give you a *good intuitive feeling* for the future outcome.

There will be *failures*, but the *successes* will greatly outnumber the failures, by at least a 4 to 1 ratio.

Once it's realized that shorter rolls greatly exceed the longer rolls, then you are on the way to profitable playing.

PROFITS

WITH

PLEASURE

It will be best to chart, Super-chart and Mega-chart, and you must chart to earn consistent profits.

Charting is to compile the continuous flow of numbers generated by everyone.

Super-charting is maintaining a running total of Sevens (7's) as compared to **all the numbers.** Theoretically, one-sixth of all the numbers generated will be a Seven (7).

Mega-charting is keeping a running total **of the inside numbers (5, 6, 8, 9)** and comparing this with the running total of all numbers. Theoretically, one-half of all the numbers created by the DICE will be inside munbers (5, 6, 8, 9).

The principle attached to all phases of charting is that "in time" everything should be what is expected, as per the 36 Probability Table.

During fifteen years of charting, it is clear that within a reasonable time (up to two hours) these numbers have a pattern. They are askew, either above or below what the probability table predicts. Then they are in "tune" as per the probability table. Once they are on "target" as predicted, the inevitable occurs - they are askew again, or out of balance. This is an ongoing situation: On target - out of balance - on target - out of balance, etc.

Ninety-five (95 %) percent of the time this will occur within a reasonable time. The other five (5 %) percent of the time the erratic numbers go off in a tangent. The onslaught of too many 7's make the chart appear erotic or even erosive.

By coping intelligently with the 95 % element of time, earnings can be consistently maintained,

BUT

even during the other 5 % time element, earnings can be maintained, but at a much slower pace ! ! !

Even at a very, very ice cold table *earnings can be maintained if your charting is properly interpreted*. It can be done. It is being done. No one else at the table is smiling (right bettors), because no one else at the table is charting.

We must take a disadvantage in life and turn it into an advantage. Charting will do this — exchange an erratic flow of numbers into profits.

Look at your various charts, before you delve into the financially crunching world of CRAPS.

Analyze your charts when playing. If you are going to succeed you must have

PATIENCE,
DISCIPLINE,
LACK OF GREED

and a bit of intelligence- not mathematical or scientific - just plain ole' common sense and street sense.

The ocean of CRAPS is yours to swim, wade or drown ! ! !
Think - but use your head.

Above all don't be greedy. Be disciplined ! ! !

In addition to **Patience, Discipline,** and **Lack of Greed** you, as a potential provider of profits, must add that all important blending ingredient:

INTUITION

SUPER-CHARTING 7's

Super-Charting is compiling on an ongoing basis the number of 7's generated by those excitable DICE, in comparison to the total numbers generated.

Chapters can be written on the importance of super-charting 7's. Over the long period of time the total number of 7's will be approximately one-sixth of all the numbers generated by the DICE. For the short term DICE created numbers are chaotic, erratic and even erotic.

It is with the present action that we are concerned. Sometimes the 7's are on target equaling one-sixth of the total numbers. Other times there are too many sevens, primarily at the wrong time for right bettors. Rarely are the 7's scarce.

By watching the ratio of 7's as compared to the total numbers we can *increase* our profits.

A most important result of observing the 7's has permitted this author to leave a "warm" table that is about to turn "cold." Losers try to find "hot" tables or "hot" rolls to recapture part of their losses. I leave profit making tables that are primed to turn "cold" to seek the more available "normal" CRAP tables.

Profits are best obtained at "normal" tables, less likely at "hot" tables when using Zeke's techniques. This is obvious because if one or two place bet wins is our goal per shooter, we are out in left field if a shooter has five, eight, ten or more inside place bet numbers numbers. I care less.Read articles later in this book that PROVE two wins are more profitable than five inside place bet wins.

The best part of super-charting combined with mega-charting is that **PROFITS** continue on what losers call "cold" tables.

Basically profits increase at a faster rate on "normal" tables and "cold" tables. The rare "hot" rolls and "hot" tables leave me as a spectator after the quota of one or two Place Bet wins. I am leery of these tepid conditions because of the equilibrium principle.

The best tool available to act as a catalyst for super-charting is your own intuition.

Let the perpetual losers seek out the long rolls or "hot" table. I'll take the "normal" or even "cold" tables for profiteering.

Lead not your wagers into temptation.

Glance read the charts.

Don't be Greedy, have patience.

MEGA-CHARTING

Mega-Charting takes a few seconds per shooter's roll. It is simply maintaining a running total of the inside (5, 6, 8, 9) numbers. There are eighteen ways to make these inside numbers, or *ONE-HALF* of the 36 numbers possible.

Glance reading the ongoing running total and comparing this total to the total numbers generated gives you an excellent feeling on how and when to wager, or increase or decrease wagers.

Mega-Charting only succeeds when guided by the super-charting. If a normal rate of 7's (one-sixth ratio) **exists** then the ratio of the inside numbers (5, 6, 8, 9) is the prevailing factor. If the inside numbers is less than one half, loosen ye' wallets. When the ratio is abnormally higher than one-half and the 7's are normal are less than one-sixth, tread lightly. This is fun time, because your intuition is an additional guiding force. The over-riding factor is always the ratio of the 7's.

The inside numbers (5, 6, 8, 9) ratio only comes into play when the 7's ration are normal or higher than normal.

THE CRITICAL DECISION MAKER FOR MEGA-CHARTING IS THE VALUES OF 7's.

THE HIGHER THE RATIO OF 7's ABOVE ONE-SIXTH AVERAGE, THE BETTER THE OPPORTUNITY FOR EARNING PROFITS.

These are exceptions when the inside numbers ratio is exceptionally LESS than one-half. In defiance of the 7's ratio, I exploited the situation for additional wins. So can you. Let your own intuition be your guide to success. Be careful not to allow your intuition instincts to be overworked, or "burnt out".

CHARTING PAD FORMAT

Casino	Taj Mahal		Date 5-20	Start 2:10	End	

L	W	1	2	3	4	5	6	7	8	9	10	11	12	13	14	15	16	17	Inside #	7's	Total #
L		⑧	3	2	6	9	7												3	1	6
L		7	⑨	5	10	10	8ₕ	7ₒₜ											6	3	13
L		④	11	7															–	4	16
	W	12	⑥	8	6														9	–	20
L		⑤	3	9	3	7ₙₛ													11	5	25
L		⑩	8	5	7														13	6	29
	W	11	⑤	4	5														15	–	33
	W	⑨	5	9															18	–	36

Designations:

⑨   Circled number is point number   OT   Off Table

H   Hardways 4, 6, 8 & 10   CS   Corner Shooter

NS   New Stickperson   PS   Pre-Set Shooter

DD   Dropped DIE or DICE

A pre-printed 4″ x 6″ charting pad that has provisions for charting, super-charting and mega-charting is available. This easy to use pad also contains Zeke's techniques and charting samples.

Contact:
Hi-Lo-Yo Publishing Company
P.O. Box 711
Skippack, PA 19474-0711

BEWARE OF OTHER CRAP SHOOTERS

This is a most important subject for the journey onward to earn *profits* in the stimulating 'Arena of CRAP Action'.

During an average one-hour of CRAP play, there will be approximately 130 to 140 numbers sired by those exhilarating jumpin' dominoes. Every 36 numbers will average 6 - 7's over the time you are at the CRAP Tables. This means approximately one-sixth of all the numbers generated will be a 7. They can appear rather frequently, generally on target, and rarely infrequently — but generally averaging one-sixth of the numbers thrown .

Therefore we can expect 22 to 24 - 7's every hour of CRAP play. I have experienced bypassing at least three to four 7's per hour by watching the shooter's 'modus operandi'.

Some of the techniques border on superstition, others are based on facts. Superstition or not, these techniques are worthwhile and worked to my advantage, and should work for you also.

Avoid CRAP shooters who use the following techniques in tossing the DICE:

(1) Tosses the DICE into either of the front corners of the furthest wall. There is no logical or mathematical basis for this but this type shooter's technique breeds 7's.

(2) Tosses the DICE nonchalantly, as if with no interest in the outcome.

(3) Sharply tosses DICE into front wall.

(4) Shooter takes an inordinate amount of time in creating his specific pre-set of the DICE.

The above appears to have a superstitious approach, nevertheless my experiences warrants *"off all bets - no action"*.

Factually, there are various type DICE pre-sets that breed 7's. This is because the shooters pre-sets will alter the 36 Probability Table.

Please note carefully that under present conditions of tossing the DICE against the special padded front wall the DICE bounce back in all directions. The days of yore when we had sophisticated CRAP shooters who merely tossed the DICE against a flat wall, or on a flat surface generating desired numbers, are completely gone.

DICE mechanics are a thing of the past, but this is my theory regarding altering the outcome of tossed DIE.

I repeat, altering the 36 Probability or 36 Frequency Table is not a definite control of the DICE. By 'altering' the DICE it is meant - altering or changing the amount of a given number from its frequency pattern. Example would be having a specific pre-set of the DICE that would increase the amount of 7's per 36 numbers from 6 times to 8 or 9 times. This is an increase of 33 % to 50 % giving a tremendous advantage when shooting on the come out roll. Beware of the wrong bettors with pre-sets that breed 7's.

Back to basics. In the long term of playing time, it is suggested that when a shooter uses a pre-determined pre-set of the DICE that have a CRAP number on the top surfaces (2, 3, 12) then instruct the dealer IMMEDIATELY before the DICE leaves the shooter's hands: "NO ACTION." or "OFF ! ! !"

For this contract between you and the casino to be valid, the dealer must respond by repeating "No Action" or "Off".

The best way to handle this is to observe the shooter's 'modus-operandi' BEFORE making any wagers. Generally speaking, even though there is a continuous change in the players, the majority of players would be present during your period of play at a particular table. Again, observe and make your decision to wager in sufficient time, depending on your personal intuitive opinion regarding shooter's tossing techniques.

What does this do for you ? If you as a player can *avoid* three to four 7's in this manner per hour, then you have avoided approximately 15 % of the 7's that can financially hurt you.

CRAPS for the Place Bettor is really a guessing game. You are continuously attempting to obtain a ratio between wins and losses of 4 to 1.

When wagering on the inside numbers (4, 5, 6, 9) for a minimum of $22 or any multiple of $22 such as $44, $66, $88, $110, $220, $330 etc. whenever a losing 7 causes your inside place wagers to come tumbling down, it will take 3.14 wins to offset this loss.

$$\frac{\$22}{7} = 3.14$$

Please note this is the mathematical value of PI (π).

KEENLY OBSERVE PRE-SETS
(worthwhile repeating)

On your path to **profits,** you will need every tool available to avoid that financially ruinous 7. It only takes one 7 to send your stack of place bet chips tumbling down, only to be reassembled in the dealer's collection.

Your knowledge of DICE mechanics is to permit you **not** to wager on the place bets when the shooter pre-sets the DICE on certain values (setting of the DICE).

When a CRAP shooter deliberately pre-sets the DICE on any seven (1-6, 2-5, 3-4) **do not** make any place bets.

If the pre-sets (top surfaces) are set on any CRAP number (2, 3, 12) **do not** make any place bets.

There will be exceptions, but in the long run you will be better off. After all, our goal is a **minimum** of four place bet wins to every losing 7.

By observing the shooters 'modus-operandi' you will increase your chances of creating a profit. Don't be upset if there are exceptions where the shooter's wins outweigh the one devilish 7 by factors exceeding five-to-one. In the final analysis, you will tremendously increase your profits if you generally avoid certain DICE pre-sets.

You are probably wondering why the 11 pre-set was not included in this category ? Simple answer. Two of this authors pre-sets, for more place bet numbers than theoretically expected, have the pre-set value of 11 on the top two surfaces of the DICE. In addition the very two the longest shooter's rolls that I personally witnessed had the 11 on the top two surfaces.

CASINOS DEVOUR OVER
34 % OF CRAP BANKROLL

"MISTAKEN IDENTIFICATION"

The New Jersey Casino Commission together with all Atlantic City Casinos unwittingly erred in calculating the true Casino's win percentage for CRAPS,

The data obtained by the drop and win figures gives the commission a basis for reference. However, I state that the Casino's real win percentage is higher than published.

By simple arithmetic, we can show that there is a "duplication" of dollar drop. The Casino's dollar win divided by a lower correct dollar drop would result in a higher Casino win percentage in CRAPS.

Let's think about this for a moment.

Assume that a typical player exchanges $200 for chips. After playing CRAPS for two hours, lets suppose it may be time for lunch or dinner. The run-of-the-mill player goes to the cashier's cage and exchanges the chips for $80 or $280 in currency depending on wether he was ahead or behind. Why carry around dirty, heavy chips when temporarily leaving the casino ?

After eating something light, the player returns to the CRAP Action Arena and exchanges possibly $100 or $200 for chips. Now what do we have ? If the player never exchanged chips for currency until the very end of play, be it at the end of one session, one day, one weekend, or as long as he or she is a player — then the dollar drop would be lower. Think about it !

Sometimes players will cash-in their chips to change their luck.

I am certain that you as a reader can offer more times when chips are exchanged for currency:

Security Reasons	Massage Time
Snack Time	Rest Periods
Fitness Room Visits	Show Time
Swim Time	etc.

After talking with key casino executives, I find that it is a practice among some players with higher credit limits to ask for a sizable marker, possibly play for a short period of time and then leave the casino. In this manner the player has obtained an interest free loan.

One of the casinos top credit executives told me of a prominent Atlantic City businessman who obtained a marker for $25,000. Then proceeding immediately to the cashier's cage to cash-in. Thus easily securing an interest free "loan".

Apparently this is more common that I expected. I also was informed that many players frequently cash in their chips for fresh money. They hope to give the impression to the casino people that they are investing more money so they can obtain larger comps. These two examples certainly add to the false dollar drop figures, and according to top knowledgeable executives, the dollar drop is dramatically affected by these false dollar drops.

Information obtained from casino executives was encouraging. One source estimated this duplication at about 30 %. Six other sources stated it ranged from 20 % to 25 %. These estimates were in the proper direction, but low ! ! !

NEW JERSEY CASINO CONTROL COMMISSION RESULTS

1991 Recorded CRAPS Drop	=	$ 2,275,571,000
Casino's Dollar Win	=	$ 348,872,000
Casino's Win Percentage	=	15.33 %

AUTHOR'S EVALUATION

The average typical CRAP player's time would be one daily session.

During a four months period, I spoke to over four hundred players. These conversations took less than two minutes each. The following analysis was predicated on a typical 100 CRAP players.

Question:

"Normally how many times during a day do you cash in your chips for any reason such as meal time showtime or breaktime ?"

Analysis:

Players	Extra trip to Cash In	False Drops
34	0	0
27	1	27
21	2	42
14	3	42
3	4	12
1	5	5
100		128

Let's assume, for simplicity, that these 100 typical CRAP players initially purchased $100 in chips. Now a break is needed. It may be that he or she may be down $30 to $40 or up possibly $20 to $80. It really does not matter. If player A is down $27 and received $73 for his or her chips, it is almost a certainty that upon returning to the casino another $100 bill will be tendered for chips. If player B won $61 and received $161 for the chips, it is again a certainty that he will also tender $100 for chips when re-entering the Arena of CRAP Action.

An area worth discussing is the larger player who has dedicated $1000 to $5000 as his CRAP bankroll. To obtain potential comps this player may tender this money or marker at the outset of play. But as time and DICE take their toll, the CRAP bankroll will continuously dwindle. Therefore after exchanging chips for paper currency or reduction of a marker, two things will occur. Most likely the **cash** player will tender less cash when returning to the tables. But the **marker type** character will again re-establish his comp potential by requesting the "full marker" as before.

I believe the overall difference in calculating the false drop is negligible. It is also my opinion that the bulk of drops are financed (yes, financed) by the smaller players.

So onward to our analysis.

According to our "typical 100 CRAP players" twenty-seven (27) made one additional trip to the cashiers cage besides the final trip at daily sessions end. This accounts for 27 false drops. Twenty-one (21) made two additional trips to exchange chips for currency. Obviously these 21 players account for 42 false drops. Going through the same process we have a total of 128 false drops.

Assuming this typical group each had initial drops of $100 and each following drop was of the same magnitude, we can arrive at some interesting conclusions. Yes, I will admit that portions of the false drops will be less than players original drop. But according to my poll most players re-entered our invigorating arena of action with approximately the same CRAP bankroll.

Knowing this, let's proceed:

Original CRAP bankrolls = 100 players x $100 = $10,000
Extra (false) drops = 128 x $100 = $12,800
$22,800

Casino's win based on 100 % drop for 1991 = 15.33 %
15.33 % of $22,800 = $3,495

$$\frac{\$3,495}{\text{Original } \$10,000} = 34.95 \quad \text{UGH!!!}$$

This is what the Casinos devour and consume
from the CRAP players bankroll ! ! !

This is no reflection on the casinos or the New Jersey Casino Control Commission. There is no accurate method to exactly measure the duplication of dollar drop. The information is only presented to let the public know that the **Casino's True Win Percentage On Craps Is Higher By Over 100% than Indicated.**

DECREASING PERCENTAGES

What goofballs we have in the Arena of CRAP Action ! ! !

This includes most authors, most so-called CRAP experts, and almost everyone involved in the game of CRAPS. Including casino personnel (from top to bottom) and those CRAP playing math wizards.

They just never understood CRAPS. John Scarne laid the groundwork. Obviously no subsequent author ever fully and completely investigated the **odds aspect** of the game, until now.

Everyone of the previous CRAP authors state that the more odds a pass line player takes, or the more odds that a wrong bettor lays, the CRAP player's quality of play increases. This is because of the decreasing Casino's win percentage.

Imagine, all of these authorities never understanding CRAPS. It's sickening ! ! !

Look at the *decreasing percentages* as the pass line player **increases risk** money to reduce the Casino's win percentage in order to maintain a constant player's dollar loss or a constant Casino dollar win. The constant loss for the player will always be 248 times the dollar value of the pass line wager **once the point number is established.** In this case $5 times 248 or $1240 per the 1320 pass line points taken place during the 14 hours (1980 tosses of the DICE), assuming a $5 pass line wager.

DECREASING PERCENTAGES

$ 1240 PASS LINE LOSS
for every $5 pass line wager
(Once Point Number is Established)

For simplification:

In over 1980 numbers generated by those mystifying DICE, the pass line point **losers** (784) **exceed** the pass line point **winners** (536) by 248.

For every $5 bet on Pass Line and Come Bet (once the point number is established) over a period of 1320 point numbers, (total of losers and winners) the pass line bettor is expected to lose $1240.

$$248 \text{ more losers} \times \$5 \text{ each bet} = \$1240.$$

$$\frac{784 \text{ losers}}{1320 \text{ total point numbers}} = \textbf{59.39 \%} \text{ Pass Line Point \textbf{Losers}}$$

$$\frac{784 \text{ losers}}{536 \text{ winners}} = \begin{array}{l} \text{1.4627 or 46.27 \% \textbf{more} Pass Line} \\ \text{Point Losers than Winners} \end{array}$$

Santa Claus for the Casino is the Pass Line and Don't Pass Line player.

DECREASING CASINO'S WIN PERCENTAGE
BUT CONSTANT CASINO DOLLAR WIN

Novice players move on to the green pastures (*Place Bets*). Let's take time to prove to those *Doubting Thomases* that what I am saying about those stupid decreasing percentages, as they relate to the increased investment of odds, are true.

No Odds:

      Investment: = 1320 Points x $ 5 = $ 6,600
      Casino's win: 1,240
      Casino's percentage: 18.79 %

Single Odds:

      Investment: = 1320 Points x $ 10 = $ 13,200
      Casino's win: 1,240
      Casino's percentage: 9.39 %

Double Odds:

      Investment: = 1320 Points x $ 15 = $ 19,800
      Casino's win: 1,240
      Casino's percentage: 6.26 %

Triple Odds:

      Investment: = 1320 Points x $ 20 = $ 26,400
      Casino's win: 1,240
      Casino's percentage: 4.70 %

Five x Odds:

      Investment: = 1320 Points x $ 30 = $ 39,600
      Casino's win: 1,240
      Casino's percentage;   3.13 %

One Hundred x Odds:

      Investment: = 1320 Points x $505 = $666,600
      Casino's win: 1,240
      Casino's percentage: 0.186 %

SUMMARY:

For every dollar wager on the Pass Line, the casino expects to win 248 times this amount over the course of the 1320 pass line point numbers, once point number is established.

I admit that sometimes "hot streaks" appear. After reviewing my personal charts over the past ten years, they reveal that the pass line losers exceed the pass line winners by more than 69 %, instead of the expected 46 %. This fact appeared approximately 65 % of the time . The other 35 % of the time tends to balance the scale.

If you, as a player, are maximizing the "free odds" opportunity, you will be without funds very quickly. True the opposite can occur, but I have no scientific basis to say this but from historical experience, **it won't happen !**

WORTH REPEATING

Pass Line Percentages

Once the pass line point number is established, then, at this very instant, the casino's win percentage is 18.79 %. Not what most authorities believe it to be, 1.414 %. The reason they have the low 1.414 % is due to the tremendous two-to-one win factor during the Come Out Rolls. Over a time period (about 14 hours or 1980 tosses), assuming that the pass line player is always wagering on the come out roll, the pass line will lose 28 times more often than it wins. On the come-out-roll, the pass line wager will win 440 times while losing 220 times, as indicated on the1980 Probability Table. **This tremendous come-out-roll advantage breeds 220 net wins.**

Hell freezes over once the point number is established. From the 1980 Probability Table, there will be 1320 point numbers, of which 784 pass line point numbers are doomed for failure, and 536 pass line point numbers will succeed. This is why the pass line is a HORRENDOUS WAGER once the point number is established.

Pass Line Point Number Losses	784
Pass Line Point Number Wins	- 536
Net Point Number Losses	248
Net Come-Out-Roll Wins	- 220
Net Pass Line LOSSES	28

Hence the casino's overall win percentage for the pass line with no odds is:

$$\frac{28 \text{ Net Losses}}{1980 \text{ Total Numbers}} = 1.414 \%$$

Note: At the instant that a pass line point number is established, the Casino's win percentage is 18.79 % _not_ 1.414 % as most players and experts believe.

The 18.79 % casino's win percentage is a weighted percentage.

Individually, the casino's win percentage is:

Point Number	Casino's Win Percentage
4 or 10	33.33 %
5 or 9	20.00 %
6 or 8	9.09 %

You can see why I must call the other authors unknowledgeable !

Note: $\dfrac{248 \text{ Pass Line Point Losers}}{1320 \text{ Point Numbers}} = 18.79 \%$

$\dfrac{18.788 \%}{1.414 \%} = 13.3$ times larger

RESULTS of "FREE ODDS" AFTER PASS LINE NUMBER IS ESTABLISHED

Casino's Percentages

Numbers	No Odds	Single Odds	Double Odds	Five x Odds	Ten x Odds
4 or 10	33.3	16.7	11.1	5.56	3.03
5 or 9	20.0	***10.0	6.67	3.33	1.82
6 or 8	9.09	4.5	3.03	1.515	0.826

In all cases above the casino's dollar return remains constant per table below. This means that for the *total number of events* the Casino Dollar Return is a function of the Pass Line number.

* Events	Numbers	** Casino Dollar ($) Return
3 + 6 = 9	4 & 10	3 x Pass Line bet
4 + 6 = 10	5 & 9	2 x Pass Line bet
5 + 6 = 11	6 & 8	1 x Pass Line bet

* Events = Ways to win PLUS ways to lose.

** For number of events

*** For Single Odds, 10.0 % is the correct Casino's percentage when the Pass Line bet equals the single odds bet. But if Pass Line bet is $5 and the odds bet is $6 the Casino's percentage decreases to 9.09 %. This is because the single odds wager is 20 % larger than the $5 Pass Line wager.

ZEKE'S TECHNIQUES

1. For earning PROFITS *only* wager on the place bets.

2. *Never press Place bets*

3. Best bet would be one hit (win) and complete removal of all place bets, preferably the inside numbers of 5, 6, 8 and 9. Then wait for new shooter for next wager.

4. Add insurance factor by charting.

5. Add additional insurance by super-charting. Super-charting is the compiling and comparing the total number of 7's to the total numbers rolled (including 7's). Theoretically, the 7's should be one-sixth of the total numbers.

6. Mega-charting adds an important flavor of insurance. Mega-charting is keeping a running total of inside numbers (5, 6, 8, 9) as compared to total numbers generated. Mega-charting is only effective when Super-charting indicates that future rolls could be low in 7's. Inside numbers (5, 6, 8, 9) theoretically should be one-half of total numbers.

7. Increase value of place bets only after win at beginning of new shooter, when suggested by Chart, Super-chart and Mega-chart.

8. **Never play Pass Line unless shooting DICE.** When shooting

(as in fun time, etc.) place at least three place bets. If equipped with proper pre-set, then possibly go for two or more wins.

9. Avoid proposition bets except for fun time, pre-set time and intuitive time.

10. Five place bets when chart approved are superb bets. Be careful about second or more wins. Suggest removal of first hit place bet, then remove each successive win. If removed bets are generated again then remove balance of place bets. Financial risk is greater than normal, be very very careful. Only place five wagers when ahead ! ! !

11. Historical charting shows that if place bet is not won within a given number of tosses, it is wise to remove all place bets. This given number can range from five to seven depending upon charting and intuitive feeling. Given numbers include every number from beginning of roll, including numbers before establishing point number.

12. There is no scientific reason for this, but if first three numbers of new shooter are craps, sevens or elevens (any combination) this author has gained by not making any Place bets. My personal records for the past 15 years indicate that the odds against any point number being made exceeds 5 to 1. Now you know this should not be the case, but for me it works.

13. Omitted for superstitious reasons.

14. Place bets on all six numbers (4, 5, 6, 8, 9 AND 10) are

superior bets for one, two, and three possible hits when chart approved. Suggest removal of place bets that are won. If removed place bet is hit again, then remove remaining place bets. Intuition and charting should help in decision. **Very risky, even for the experienced player.** It is preferred to opt for two wins on the four inside numbers (5, 6, 8, 9).

15. When place bets have higher dollar value than your normal wager and you are attempting a second win, **it is strongly suggested** that you reduce dollar amount for second attempt. Also remove place bet that is won, or at least reduce dollar value on winning place bet.

16. **Remove all Place wagers if any of the following occurs:**

    (1) One or both dice leave the CRAP table.
    (2) The shooter drops one DIE or both DICE.
    (3) A new stickperson replaces the previous stickperson.
    (4) The shooter throws the DICE nonchalantly with no sincerity.
    (5) The shooter changes one or both DICE.
    (6) The shooter whips DICE with much more than normal force against back wall.
    (7) Shooter aims for either corner of back wall.
    (8) Any time that player feels intuitively that the ugly seven is due.

17. Pass Line betting time.
    (a) Fun Time
    (b) Superstitious Time
    (c) Intuitive Time

18. **Never** chase a consecutive series of shooter's losing rolls without any inside numbers (5, 6, 8 and 9) appearing before the ugly seven, after new point number is established.
This inside number (5, 6, 8, or 9) must appear within three additional tosses after establishing point number

19. **Never** increase Place bets after a loss.

20. **Never** make Place bets in the middle of an unknown roll.

21. When properly increasing dollar value of place bets, chart and intuition may suggest increasing certain place bets selectively above basic increase. Definitely when any of these numbers are hit and won, remove this number completely and again reduce dollar value of other place bets. Sometimes I benefit leaving wagers on the 6 AND 8, no matter if one of these was hit already.

22. **Never** work Place bets on the come out roll.

23. **Never** wager on the family of Don't Pass Bets and Don't Come Bets.

24. **Never** wager on the family of Pass Line Bets and Come Bets. When you are a shooter, play Pass Line but *no* Come bets. Taking odds is a preference of Pre-set and intuition. (Six months later, after comfortably earning an income.)

25. An excellent technique when playing the inside place bets on the 5, 6, 8 and 9; if 5 or 9 is made (won) then remove both the 5 & 9 and let the 6 & 8 remain. If the 6 **or** 8 is hit then remove **both** the 6 and 8. **IMPORTANT:** If 5 or 9 is repeated again, remove **both** the 6 and 8.

26. **Avoid** Place bets on the 4 or 10. Even when chart approved and good intuitive feeling, it is a gamble - a very low percentage of earning any income.

VERY IMPORTANT:

Whenever you approach ANY CRAP TABLE, chart and observe the numbers generated by the DICE for at least 10 minutes. This would be a minimum of 22 numbers.

HORRENDOUS WAGERS ! ! !

- Pass Line
- Don't Pass Line
- Come Bet
- Don't Come Bet
- Vigorish to Buy 4 or 10
- Place Bets 4 or 10
- Odds Behind Pass Line
- Laying Odds for Wrong Bettor
- Pressing *Any* Place Bets

The above imbecilic stupid CRAP play accounts for over 92 % of the casino's dollar win at CRAPS.

Casino CRAPS cannot be BEAT as suggested by *other authors, so called crap experts* or *gambling authorities.*

Please explain to me why there are less than one percent overall CRAP winners. Could it be because every book written on how to win at CRAPS or Beat the Casino repeats the same smelly garbage? Some attempt cute-sy plays, and others try money management. When, in the final analysis the success rate winning at CRAPS is less than one percent. And these winners did not learn anything from the "experts". They combined street-sense with common sense to become self-taught.

You should be angry, embittered and disgusted that you followed the CRAP cowpath of previous players and authors. A winning success rate of only one percent (and those were probably SELF-TAUGHT) suggested *pit-falls* with other playing methods.

I am also irritated. Education, in any subject matter, should enable you to go further in life to newer heights — *not* directing you to the FINANCIAL SEWER ! ! !

Today, the success rate for winners in the Arena of CRAP Action is LESS than one (1%) percent.

The success rate of my readers should greatly exceed twenty (20 %) percent. This rate is more than twenty times greater than present day winners.

Failures will result *not* because of the call of the wild (stickman's call), but because people are basically *greedy*. They want one more place bet win, sometimes after a full press. Or they *lack patience*. Combined, these faults will exist because of *no self discipline*.

This twenty-plus percent success rate could be much higher. High enough to force the luxurious casinos to change CRAP odds in order to continue making a profit in the Hippodrome of CRAP Action.

The rate of CRAP success will not increase because of human nature:

GREED

LACK OF PATIENCE

LACK OF DISCIPLINE

Even those that fail will recognize it was not because of the call of the wild (stickman's call of the DICE numbers generated). Honest thinking losers will admittedly blame themselves in disgust. Some will retrench and go back to basics, most will not ! ! !

THIS IS WHY PLACE BETTORS ARE LOSERS !

Two Wins Are More Profitable Than Five Wins
Two Wins Are Better Than Six Wins

This is very intriguing. There is a mathematical basis for making such a statement. Let's first assume using the four inside numbers (5, 6, 8, 9), each with the minimum wager ($22 total), we have been on target chart-wise and have recorded two wins so far. At the point of the second win, the profit for this shooter is two times $7 or $14.

If we now remove our four inside wagers, our $14 profit for this shooter is clearly protected. Let's project into the future what would happen if we permitted our $22 investment to remain as we go for broke:

Win #	Profit Including This Win	Net Income if 7 Before next Win	
3	$ 21	Loss	$ 1
4	$ 28	Profit	$ 6
5	$ 35	Profit	$ 13
6	$ 42	Profit	$ 20

This projection should help us take a positive posture. The most serious decision a CRAP player has when he is pressing his place bets is *when should he completely remove or decrease dollar value of Press Bets.* This is really a dilemma ! !

Let's relate this to the fortunate profiteer who has two wins for a $14 profit if the inside (5, 6, 8, 9) place bets are removed.

This is clearly the only decision our income earner can make if the goal is to become a consistent winner.

Be content with two wins, a profit of $14. If greedy for the elusive long inside number rich roll, after three additional wins on the inside numbers (5, 6, 8, 9) and then a loss of $22, the profit would have decreased to $13. Going for four additional wins profit will increase from $14 to $20 if a destructive seven then appears.

I repeat - going for three additional wins (total of five) and then the 7's pops up. This reduces the $14 profit to $13.

Four additional wins, and then a non-removal of place bets, results in a total profit for this shooter of $20 when the 7 appears.

Good gosh ! Five wins for less profit than two wins ($13 instead of $14).

Gosh by golly ! Six total wins (or four wins more than two wins) increases profits from $14 to $20. But you must travel through hell avoiding 7's for four additional wins for a mere increase of only $6.

You make this simple decision. Same dilemma as the Place Bet Presser. ***When do you remove the place bets or decrease risk ?***

My solution: Go easy. The casino wants you to give them time with the action so they can tempt you with comps. These comps will grind you down and out. Obviously you want to grind the Casino for your just reward.

This analysis is very basic and simple. Never before disclosed or discussed by any previous author. It is just an added event why there are less than 1 % overall winners in the exhilarating Hippodrome of CRAP Action.

WHEN PLACE BETTING ALL SIX NUMBERS

TWO WINS ARE MORE PROFITABLE THAN SIX WINS

AND BETTER THAN SEVEN WINS

Win #	Profit Including This Win	Net Income if 7 Before next Win
1	$ 7.50	Loss $ 24.50
2	$ 15.00	Loss $ 17.00
3	$ 22.50	Loss $ 9.50
4	$ 30.00	Loss $ 2.00
5	$ 37.50	Win $ 5.50
6	$ 45.00	Win $ 13.00
7	$ 52.50	Win $ 20.50

Let's analyze the above chart.

The dilemma of the CRAP player ! ! !

When, oh when, should we remove our Place Bets ?

The answer is very obvious. Enjoy two wins for a $ 15 profit and ***then remove all Place bets.*** Now we have protected the $ 15 profit for this shooter. Going for broke, after four more wins (making a total of six wins), only gives you a net win of $ 13. This is $ 2 LESS than only two wins. Can this be ? Let me say it again: going for broke, or letting the six place bets (4, 5, 6, 8, 9, 10) remain active until the deadly singular 7 shows up, is not a good idea. We are much better off with two wins than six wins. In fact, if the Gods Of Fate would favor us with seven wins, our net gain would only be $20.50 or $5.50 more than only two wins.

Soon to be published is my book on "Casino CRAPS — Probabilities and Odds", which contains some really fascinating information.

Without delving into derivations, allow me merely to present certain facts about the probability of two wins, six wins and seven wins for the six place bets (4, 5, 6, 8, 9,10).

* Number of Wins	Probability	Odds to Win	Odds Against Winning
2	0.64000	**1.78	
6	0.26214		**2.81
7	0.20972		3.77

* Before the fatal seven.
** Odds to one.

Besides the practicality of earning more with two wins than with six wins on our six place bets, another sound reason for two wins rather than six or seven wins is found when analyzing the results of the probabilities of these wins. The probabilities of two wins, six wins and seven wins converts into the odds of making two wins and the odds against making six and seven wins.

It's great knowing the odds of winning two times on the six Place bets is in our favor (1.78 to 1), but the odds against six wins are 2.81 **against** our favor. For seven wins the odds **against** this occurring are 3.77 to 1.

This is one of the reasons why CRAP players end up in the financial CRAP-per.

Allow me to digress. Almost 18 months ago, when I began compiling articles about this very fascinating game of CRAPS, I learned some interesting facts. One of my first new disclosures was that by combining various place bets the casino's win percentages decreased dramatically. To obtain an opinion how the unknowing gambling public, authors and CRAP experts would react to my new findings, I presented my calculations to one of the most renowned casino executives. He brought along an expert on various table games, especially CRAPS. After reviewing my presentation, they both agreed: "Zeke, these are only numbers. What do numbers have to do with those crazy DICE ?"

I REST MY CASE.

36 PROBABILITY TABLE

Number	Possibilities
2	1
3	2
4	3
5	4
6	5
7	6
8	5
9	4
10	3
11	2
12	1

36 COMBINATIONS

**Two Six Sided Cubes Can Generate
36 Different Combinations of Numbers**

From the 36 Probability Table we create the 1980 Probability by multiplying 36 x 55 to obtain 1980. This is the smallest number to obtain the various **Casino's win percentages** on every possible CRAP wager without using fractions.

Right Bettor's 1980 Probability Table

Come Out Rolls	Winners	Losers
Eleven (11)	110	
Seven (7)	330	
Two (2)		55
Three (3)		110
Twelve (12)		55

Come Out Rolls = 440 + 220 = 660

Point Numbers

Point Numbers	Winners	Losers
Four (4)	55	110
Ten (10)	55	110
Five (5)	88	132
Nine (9)	88	132
Six (6)	125	150
Eight (8)	125	150

Points = 536 + 784 = 1320
1980

Total Losses = 220 + 784 = 1004
Total Wins = 440 + 536 = 976

Excess Losses = 28

$\frac{28}{1980} = 1.414\%$ **Casino's win percentage** for Pass Line and Come Bet wagers

Wrong Bettor's 1980 Probability Table

Come Out Rolls		**Winners**	Losers
Eleven	(11)		110
Seven	(7)		330
Two	(2)	55	
Three	(3)	110	
*Twelve	(12)	*Stand-off*	___

Come Out Rolls = 165 + 440 = 605

Point Number

Point		Winners	Losers
Four	(4)	110	55
Ten	(10)	110	55
Five	(5)	132	88
Nine	(9)	132	88
Six	(6)	150	125
Eight	(8)	150	125

Points = 784 + 536 = 1320

1925 *

Total Losses = 440 + 536 = 976
Total Wins   = 165 + 784 = 949

Excess Losses = 27

$\frac{27}{1925}$ = 1.40259 % **Casino's win percentage** for Don't Pass Line and Don't Come wagers

* (1980) - 55 for standoff #12 = 1925 *

CRAPS

ZEKE'S BEST BETS

Place Bets	Casino's %	Players Insurance Factor (wins / losses)
6-8	1.042	1.67
* 5-6-8-9	1.136	3.00
5-6-8	1.176	2.33
9-6-8	1.176	2.33
** 5-6-8-9	1.181	3.00
*** 4-5-6-8-9-10	1.250	4.00
**** 4-5-6-8-9-10	1.296	4.00
5-6-9	1.645	2.17
5-8-9	1.645	2.17

* When wagers are multiples of $ 22 total for all inside numbers

** When wagers are multiples of $ 30 for each of the inside numbers

*** When wagers are multiples of $ 32 total for all numbers

**** When wagers are multiples of $ 30 for each of the numbers

REMOVE ALL PLACE BETS AFTER (1) WIN

CASINO'S ADVANTAGE ON EVERY POSSIBLE INDIVIDUAL CRAP BET

	Casino's Percentage
Don't Pass w D-Odds	0.459 %
Pass w D-Odds	0.606
Don't Pass w S-Odds	0.691
Don't Come w S-Odds	0.691
Pass w S-Odds	0.848
Come w S-Odds	0.848
Don't Pass	1.403
Pass	1.414
Don't Come	1.403
Come	1.414
Place Bet 6	1.515
Place Bet 8	1.515
Field, db. 2; trpl.12	2.78
Place Bet 5	4.00
Place Bet 9	4.00
Field, db. 2; dbl.12	5.56
Place Bet 4	6.67
Place Bet 10	6.67
Six	9.09
Eight	9.09
Hardway 6	9.09
Hardway 8	9.09
Hardway 4	11.11
Hardway 10	11.11
Any Crap	11.11
Eleven (16 for 1)	11.11
Three (16 for 1)	11.11
Two (31 for 1)	13.89
Twelve (31 for 1)	13.89
Eleven (15 for 1)	16.67
Three (15 for 1)	16.67
Two (30 for 1)	16.67
Twelve (30 for 1)	16.67
Seven (5 for 1)	16.67
Under 7 (1 for 1)	16.67
Over 7 (1 for 1)	16.67

All of these percentages are without the benefit of Zeke's Techniques

PASS LINE WAGERS VERSUS PLACE BETS

Compare the following casino's win percentages *once point number is established.*

WAGER		CASINO'S WIN PERCENTAGE%	
Inside Place Bets (5, 6, 8, 9)		**1.136**	
Pass Line Wager	(weighted)	18.79	No Odds
Pass Line Wager	(4 or 10)	33.33	No Odds
Pass Line Wager	(5 or 9)	20.00	No Odds
Pass Line Wager	(6 or 8)	9.09	No Odds
Pass Line Wager	(4 or 10)	16.67	Single Odds
* Pass Line Wager	(5 or 9)	10.00	Single Odds
** Pass Line Wager	(5 or 9)	9.09	Single Odds
Pass Line Wager	(6 or 8)	4.54	Single Odds
Pass Line Wager	(4 or 10)	11.11	Double Odds
Pass Line Wager	(5 or 9)	6.67	Double Odds
Pass Line Wager	(6 or 8)	3.03	Double Odds

YOUR ATTENTION, PLEASE ! ! !

Never chase a losing series of place bets by increasing dollar values of place bets. Only gambling fools would increase basic wagers by factors of two, three or four times. This will lead to financial disaster and ruination.

If a seven causes a loss to a point number *without any inside number appearing,* then **beware** of the next shooter's roll. Once a point number is established, **wait** until any inside number appears before wagering. This inside number *must appear* within three or four additional tosses.

This will avoid those typical and not too rare losses: Point, seven - point, seven - point, seven. This is one of my best techniques. It has saved me oodles of losses. If the dice have been excessively cold, only place bet the 6 and 8, irrespective of point number. If the point number is a 6 and the first inside number is the 8, it is best to still wager on the 6 and 8.

WHAT TO DO ?

My practice of play is to win one place bet and then **remove all bets.** Sometimes I will remain for two wins before removing. I try to never let my Place bets remain for the entire roll of the shooter. Even when I am the shooter.

There have been occasions when the mannerisms of a shooter are to my choosing and I may go for three wins. So far I have been more lucky than smart.

AVOID THE UNWANTED 7

I ALWAYS AVOID SHOOTERS TOSSING THE DICE AT AN
ANGLE INTO THE CORNERS

Don't ask me why, but it seems that the 7 appears more
frequently with this type shooter.

CORNER SHOOTING

This item is worth repeating. Over the years I have noticed that certain conditions breeds more than their share of 7's. During the past twelve months, I increased my notations regarding some of these conditions. Sometimes, while glance watching various sporting events, I review my notations. I can't explain it or the reasons why it happens, but there is data for me to ponder. **Let's review my analysis.**

(1) Shooters who constantly toss the DICE into the corners, or a particular corner have the rarest of rare hot streaks. Instead of generating 7's every sixth toss (on the average), the rate of 7's thrown *increases* up to an additional 40 %.

(2) These corner shooters who *whip* the DICE quickly and sharply into the corners on every toss add another factor causing the 7 to *increase* up to 50 % more often. No explanation, but true for me.

(3) If a shooter in the middle of a roll suddenly aims the next toss into a corner, the probability that a 7 will develop is higher than the one out of six ratio. No explanation, only empirical experience.

(4) Should any of the above be combined with the ingredient of a new stickperson or component like DD (dropped DICE) or OT (off table) then the 7 is surely the deadly fling of the DICE.

As an engineer and amateur mathematician, I understand my documented results are not scientifically acknowledged, but, in my superstitious world, they work for me. Perhaps other "conditions" may work for you, but if you are playing at the same table it will work for you.

I am NOT INTO HOROSCOPES, PHRENOLOGY, PHYLACTERY, VOODOOISM, etc.

BUT

What counts is that it works for me, maybe for others.

CONVERSELY

The identical procreation of SEVENS is the resultant of a dispassionate, apathetic molder of numbers, the unconcerned nonchalant shooter

Simply - it works for me.

Warning - there are always exceptions, but they are unusual.

AVOID THE
UNWANTED SEVEN

INTUITION

**At anytime you feel uneasy about any condition,
remove your bets ! ! !**

DON'T BE GREEDY

NEVER PRESS PLACE BETS!

**Increase values of Place bets at outset - when predicted
by charting or super-charting.**

Trump Taj Mahal Casino Resort
for the month of January, 1992

Casino Revenues	Authorized Units	Win	Drop	Win Percentage
Table Game				
Blackjack	99	6,268,841	39,214,052	16.0 %
Craps	30	3,524,114	21,676,496	16.3 %
Roulette	21	1,572,530	5,930,925	26.5 %
Big Six	6	237,617	475,051	50.0 %
Baccarat	4	973,237	10,495,385	9.3 %
Minibaccarat	2	514,312	2,760,984	18.6 %
Other (Red Dog & Sic Bo)	3	164,318	472,302	34.8 %
Total - Table Games	**165**	**13,254,969**	**81,025,195**	**16.4 %**
Coin Oper. Machines			Handle	
$ .05 Slot Machines	157	508,778	3,339,703	15.2 %
$ .25 Slot Machines	1,218	5,909,153	48,644,260	12.1 %
$1.00 Slot Machines	270	2,172,595	24,476,448	8.9 %
Other Slot Machines	1,089	7,547,278	83,849,353	9.0 %
Total - Coin Oper. Machines	**2,734**	**16,137,804**	**160,309,764**	**10.1 %**
Total Casino Revenues		**$ 29,392,773**		

**Look for these other exciting new books
by Zeke Feinberg
in your bookstore soon**

CASINO CRAPS - EARN $12 TO $24 PER HOUR
PLAYING CASINO CRAPS - "BEAT the
RECESSION"

CRAPS CLATTER CHATTER

CASINO CRAPS FOR HIGH ROLLERS
HARD COVER - LIMITED EDITION

CASINO CRAPS - PLACE BETS & VIGORISH

CASINO CRAPS - HORNS, WHIRLS, HI-LO-YO
CRAPS & HARDWAYS

CASINO CRAPS - WOEFUL PASS LINE BETTOR
and the PARADOX of the WRONG
BETTOR

CASINO CRAPS - For NOVICE PLAYERS
Casino Craps is NOT for GAMBLING
Casino Craps is for EXCITING
ENTERTAINMENT

CASINO CRAPS - PROBABILITIES & ODDS

CASINO CRAPS - LIVE CASINO ACTION
FINANCIAL RESULTS USING MANY
DIFFERENT METHODS

SIC BO

BEAT THE BASTARD CASINOS BY PRE-SETTING
DICE